Ax

GW01445285

in a ⌐⌐⌐⌐

*Happy reading)
Henry!*

by

Clive PiG

with illustrations by
Karen Thwaite

PiGasus Publishing UK

Published in Great Britain in 2025 by PiGasus Publishing UK.
Copyright © 2025 Clive Raymond PiGgott.

Illustrations by Karen Thwaite.
Cover and design by Andrew Kingham.
Typeset in Georgia and Providence.

A Catalogue record for this book is available from the British Library.
ISBN 978-1-7397040-1-8

Printed in the UK by CPI Books (UK) Ltd., Croydon, CR0 4YY

The paper and board used in this paperback are natural recyclable
products made from wood grown in sustainable forests.
The manufacturing processes conform to the environmental
regulations of the country of origin.

PiGasus Publishing UK
www.clivepig.co.uk

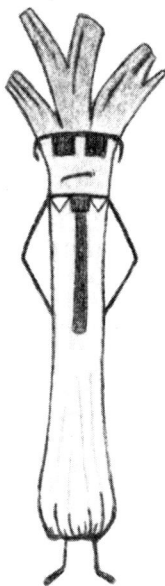

Dear Imagineers,

Like you, I just can't help it. My mind wanders.

Passing the overgrown garden of a derelict house, I spy a swing swaying beneath an apple tree bough and I wonder about the lives of those who played there long ago.

A notion is spawned. Words form. A phrase, a few lines. Rhythms, then rhymes.

I stop for a moment and jot them down in my notebook or record them on my phone.

And then, off I go, wending my merry way.

That's how it works with me. Eyes peeled, ears open. Out of the blue ideas appear, like the cow that plummeted from an aeroplane flattening poor, old Justin Case.

Later, I shape, I edit, I polish.

And that is how this glorious gallimaufry of WordPlays you hold in your hands came to be.

Poems? Lyrics? Verses? Call them what you will. They're happy just to exist. I hope you're glad they do, too.

Don't just read them. Speak them, sing them, shout them, chant them, dance them, act them.

And then create your own.

One day, I might hold your book in my hands.

Enjoy! Clive PiG

8 Axolotl in a Bottle

Axolotl In A Bottle

An axolotl in a bottle?
An ocelot in a pot?
A tortoise toddling at full throttle?
An octopus in a knot?

These are things that should not happen,
Things that should not be.
So, if you ever chance upon them,
Report it back to me.

Percy Veer

Percy Veer
Won the cup
For never ever giving up.

Not so fast,
Often last.
Never first,
Was he cursed?

He'd be lapped
Every lap.
Every relay
He'd delay.
Every hurdle
Was a hurdle.

In a sprint
He would not stint.

He'd try and try and try,
And then,
He'd trip and fall
Then rise again.

Once, lost
In the triathlon,
They sent out a search party.
They found him
In a marathon,
Last,
But hale and hearty.

The best he ever
Came was fourth,
He'd never won a medal.
No bronze, no silver nor no gold
But now he's got some metal.

Yes, Percy Veer
Won the cup
For never ever giving up.

Presented to him by his mum,
Percy was so chuffed.
He stood on the pouffe podium,
And held the prize aloft.

Mumble Grumble

If there's one thing that makes me grumble
It's when I hear a mumble.

Enunciate, don't masticate.

Don't make us wait
To hear your words.
Communicate!
Make yourself heard.

You don't have to **_SHOUT!_**
To get your ideas out!

Ears want to hear
Your great ideas.
Don't swallow them
We want to wallow in them.

Energy, not lethargy.

Get to the mouth gym,
Make sounds sing.

Ta ta ta ta tongue!
Tee tee tee tee teeth!!
La la la la lips!!!
No no no no nose!!!!
Throa throa throa throa

throat!!!!!

Don't let the cat get your tongue.
Take a deep breath,
Fill your lungs!

Let the birds out of the cage,
Make those words fly off the page.

Pop your lips,
Flick your tongue.
Show your teeth,
Let's have some fun!

Go to the mouth gym,
Words are bling.

Don't be boring
Or we'll be snoring.

Imogen's Imagination

Attention, class!
There's a serious situation.
Imogen's lost her
Imagination.

How did it happen?
She's not pleased,
She thinks it happened
When she sneezed.

Out of her mouth,
Her nose or ears?
However it happened,
It's disappeared.

Let's try and find it.
Where could it be?
Perhaps it flew up
To that tree?

In that rabbit hole?
In her socks?
Perhaps it's snuck
Behind those rocks?

Maybe its hiding from
The crowd?
Or is it floating
On that cloud?

Go and get a fishing net,
It's passing by.
Making its escape,
As a butterfly.

It's too late
It's flown away.
Perhaps it'll come back
Another day.

Poor Imogen
Has lost her powers.
Why don't we share
Some of ours?

Four Line Rhymes

String some words together
And put them in four lines.
If you're very clever
You might make some rhymes.

Silly Sausage

Sally was not silly
She ate her sausage sensibly
Unlike her sister Rose
Who stuck it up her nose.

Slow Lee

Slow Lee
Ran like a tortoise.
When we played kiss chase
He never caught us.

Awful Arthur

Arthur was an awful author,
Georgia yawned.
His stories bored her.

Terry Cotter

Terry Cotter was a potter.
Made a lotta,
Sold one notta.

Terry Cotter
Got a lotta
Terracotta.

Dad Ate My Goldfish

My parents wouldn't let me have a pet.

I wanted a goldfish.

I'd stare through the window of the pet shop
at the fish tank
but my parents would pull me away.
'They're too much trouble,' they'd say.

I won one at the fairground
but they told the stallholder to keep it
and give me a rubber duck instead.

When I got home, I filled a bowl with water
and plopped the yellow duck on top.

This gave me an idea.

I went to the pantry
and took some carrots to my room
and started to carve them
with a vegetable peeler.

It wasn't very easy,
I'm a little bit cack-handed you see.

I cut my thumb, so had to wrap a sock around it
to stop the blood dripping onto the duvet.

It took me four carrots to get the shape right.

When I put it in the bowl
I was disappointed that it only floated
beside the duck rather than sinking deeper
in the water like a real goldfish.

Still, it was better than nothing.

I introduced them to each other
and they seemed to get on very well.

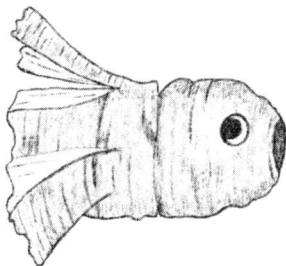

After a while, I went to the park to play football with my best friend, Ivan.

I got back just in time for dinner.

It was homemade steak and kidney pie with vegetables.

Dad laughed and lifted up his fork,
'Look at this carrot. It looks like a goldfish.'
Before I could stop him, he bit it in half.

I ran upstairs and saw the rubber duck

looking very lonely,

floating on its own

in the glass bowl.

The Crocodile Man

The Crocodile Man,
The Crocodile Man,
Beware the sharp teeth of the Crocodile Man.

Eat all the food
On your plate.
If you don't, you're rude,
That's what he hates.

He likes to snap,
He likes to trap.

He likes to snack,
He likes to crack.

He likes to bite,
He likes to tear.
He likes to fright,
Yeah, yeah, yeah, yeah!

The Crocodile Man,
The Crocodile Man,
Beware the sharp teeth of the Crocodile Man.

Eat all your food,
Especially the rice.
For your own good,
Won't tell you twice.

If he's not happy,
He gets snappy.

He's a gripper,
He's a ripper.

He like to crunch,
He likes to munch,
You'll be his lunch.

He'll chomp and chew
Then swallow you.

The Crocodile Man,
The Crocodile Man,
Beware the sharp teeth of the Crocodile Man.

So, eat all the food
On your plate.
Do what you should,
Before it's too late.

Baby Baldbeard

And so, I'm here,
But I won't be for long.
For I'm mean and I'm moody,
I'm restless and strong.

I was born in the North,
Where life's cold and it's hard.
Not soft like the life
Of the gods in Asgard.

My dad was a man
As tall as the sky
But I never did see him,
For Daddy did die

Before I was born.
Well, that was a shame,
For I've heard tales aplenty,
So great was his fame.

I was born in the winter,
And I wasn't meek.
My mum when she saw me,
Let out a big shriek!

'What is this before me?
It surely must be
The horriblest Viking
You ever did see.

Its feet are like boulders,
Its legs are like trees.
It's got the wonkiest shoulders
And the knobbliest knees.

Its stomach's as big
As the juiciest pig's.
Its chest is as bony
As the skinniest pony's.

Its hands are like crabs,
Its toes look like stumps.
On the back of his back,
There's a terrible lump.

And, as for the top,
You'll not differ to beg,
Its shiny big head ...
Well, it looks like an egg.

Its eyes blaze like fire,
Its nose snorts and fumes.
Its breath stinks of onions,
It gurgles the most abominable tunes.

It grins like a mad thing,
Have the gods played a trick?
It's terribly distressing
But he makes me feel sick.

And to top off the lot,
I've seen nothing so weird.
This terrible tot's
Got an 'orrible beard!'

Hair Today, Gone Tomorrow

Where's my hair?
It's not there!

I fell asleep in the middle of a field.
When I awoke, I could not feel
Anything upon my head.
Would this have happened if I'd stayed in bed?

Did someone have a pair of shears?
I checked, at least they'd spared my ears.

A lawnmower's lunch?
Did the cows munch?
Did birds peck it to make a nest?
A tailor use it for their Sunday best?

But I won't despair
Because I'm not a shoe without a pair.
I'm not a table without a chair.
A house without a stair.
Neither a bear without a lair,
Nor a village without a fair.

To tell the truth
I do not care.
My head will not for long be bare.

I'll just go and get a hat.
That's all folks.
Now that is that.

No, it's not.
For I forgot
To let you know
What would really make me low.

I would truly feel so weird
If I'd awoke without my beard.

Up On The Moor

Time to think,
Time to dream.
Sit on the grass,
Beside the stream.
See the sheep,
Hear the crow,
Sense those who lived here long ago.

Up on the moor, with the gorse and heather,
Buzzards soar above the tor.
Up on the moor, with the changing weather,
Miles of wilderness to explore.

When you walk along the ridge,
See the ancient clapper bridge.
Circles of stone above the ground,
Echoes of the past, all around.

Chorus ...
Up on the moor ... etc

Wild and windswept,
Cold and bleak,
Ponies stand still on the peat.
Fox and badger pass them by,
Underneath the darkening sky.

Chorus ...
Up on the moor ... etc

The Pesky Pixy

Last summer I was walking
Up upon the moor.
The sound of no-one talking
Is a sound that I adore.
I came upon a secret pool
Where I plopped in a stone,
But since I broke that silly rule
I've never been alone.

How was I to know that water
Was a boating lake
For the pixy and his daughter?
It was a mistake!
The ripples made their boat capsize
'Twas then I heard their shouts.
After I had rubbed my eyes
I pulled both pixies out.

He was so hopping angry
That soon his clothes were dry.
His voice was very squeaky,
He looked me in the eye

And said, 'For that awful incident
You will have to pay.'
I said, 'It was just an accident.'
But he won't go away.

There is a pesky pixy
Who never lets me be.
He mixes mustard in my coffee
And stirs salt into my tea.
He shakes pepper on the popcorn
And puts maggots in my cheese.
I get no sleep from dusk 'til dawn,
My bed is full of fleas.

The Whole Tooth
And
Nothing But The Tooth

I lost a tooth
And that's the truth.
But it's a lie,
I lost an eye.

And goodness knows!
I've still my nose
And my fingers
And my toes.

I beg you,
Don't believe what Greg and Meg have said,

Meg and Greg
      have
          pulled
             your
                leg.

Moor Monster

A monster lived up on the moor,
He'd romp and stomp from tor to tor.
A monster lived up on the moor,
He used to rant and rail and roar.
O Monster, Mighty Monster!
O Monster, Mighty Monster!
A monster lived up on the moor,
That was in the days of yore.

Eyes that spark,
Nose so sharp.
Claws that slash,
Paws that bash.

Every day we'd have to send,
One of us to meet their end.
It wasn't good, it wasn't nice,
To see our loved ones sacrificed.
O Monster, Mighty Monster!
O Monster, Mighty Monster!
If we refused him, he'd come down,
And stomp and smash and bash our town.

Fangs that munch,
Jaws that crunch.
Feet that crush
All to slush.

'Til one young girl, so bold and brave,
Proclaimed, 'My people, I will save!'
She took a knife, we held our breath,
She pledged she'd fight unto the death.
O Monster, Mighty Monster!
O Monster, Mighty Monster!
He gulped her down, swallowed her whole.
She ripped his belly and came out the hole.

Beware Belinda

She looks out from a dirty *winnda*
Pointing with a crooked finger.
Burning eyes like glowing cinders
Life's about to get much grimmer.

Beware Belinda
Twisted—bitter.
BeWAAAAAAAAAAAAAAAAAAAAAARE
Belinda!!!!

She drives a car with windscreen vipers
Stalking you just like a tiger.
She'll devour you for her dinner
Wash you down with neat paint thinner.

Beware Belinda
Twisted—bitter.
BeWAAAAAAAAAAAAAAAAAAAAAARE
Belinda!!!!

But you can beat her—be a winner
Be brave and try to appease her.
Touch the sadness deep within her
Make her soul look in the mirror.

Beware Belinda
Twisted—bitter.
BeWAAAAAAAAAAAAAAAAAAAARE
Belinda!!!!

If that fails and then she gets yer
Rage and scream and cuss and curse her.
Scratch and sneer and kick and taunt her
When you're dead, you're gonna haunt her.

Beware Belinda
Twisted—bitter.
BeWAAAAAAAA
AAAAAAAAAA
AAAAAAAAA
AAAAAAAA
AAAAAAA
AAAAAA
AAAAA
AARE
Belinda!!!!

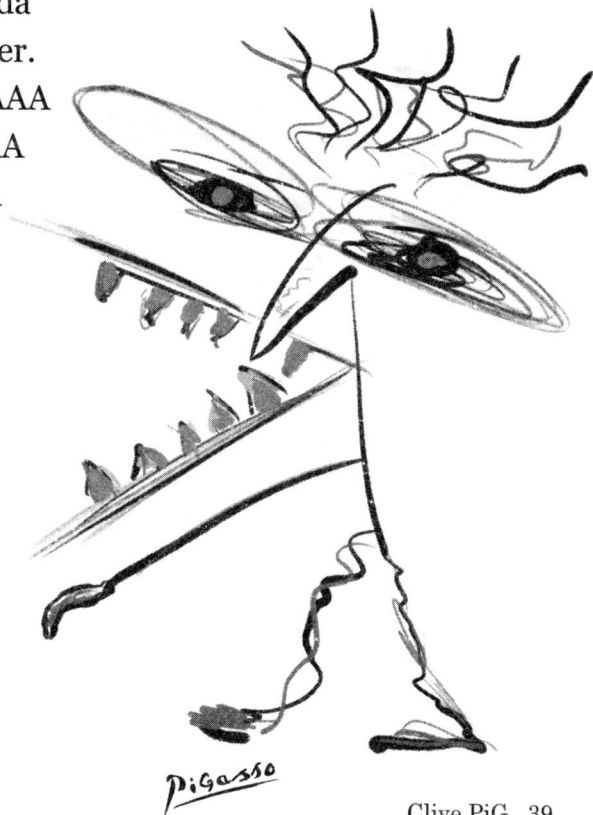

Pigasso

This Is Not A Hat

What's that?

It's not a hat!
It's a frog on a log!

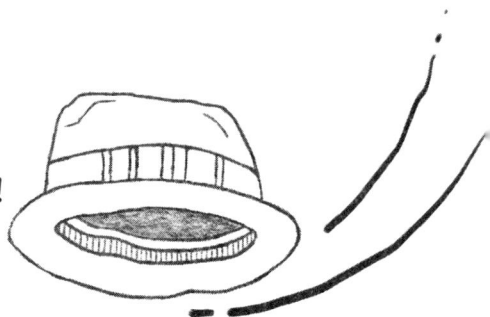

What's that?

It's not a hat.
If you can't see that
Silly you!

It's a cat.
It's a kangaroo.

It's a bowl full of stew
I can share with you.

It's a pot for a flower.
An umbrella for a shower.

What's that?

It's not a hat!

It's a deep dark hole,
Down there lives a mole.

It's a turtle's shell,
And a camel's hump as well.

It's a well,
As well.

What's that?

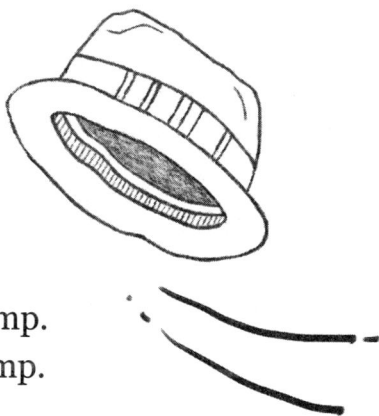

It's not a hat!
It's a bump, it's a dump.
It's a lump, it's a stump.

It's a hill, it's a mountain.
It's a lake, it's a fountain!

It drinks the rain.

A boat that floats.
It's the wheel of a train.

What's that?

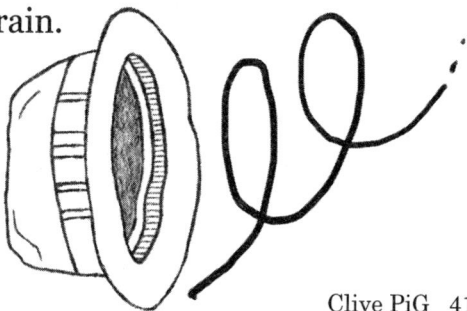

It's not a hat!

It's a brain warmer.
It's an ear tickler.
It's a hair gobbler.
It's a head polisher.

But my sister says,
'It's just a hat.'

Well, fancy that!

Ceci n'est pas un chapeau

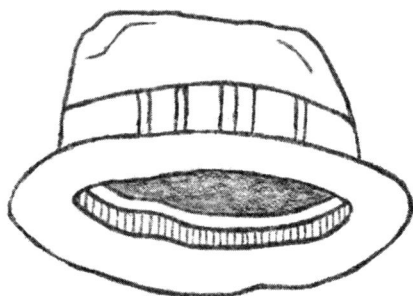

The Object Of My Desire

The object of my desire
Whose exquisiteness I so admire
You fill my heart with raging fire
Of your magnificence I'll never tire
Whose beauty doth me inspire
To make much music 'pon my lyre
Pen lyrics for a heavenly choir
To sing with skylarks, higher and higher
Above transcendent gothic spires
Causing angels to perspire
Until they ultimately require
A quiet place for to retire
Where, there some sweet soul may enquire,
'Why is this poetry so dire?'

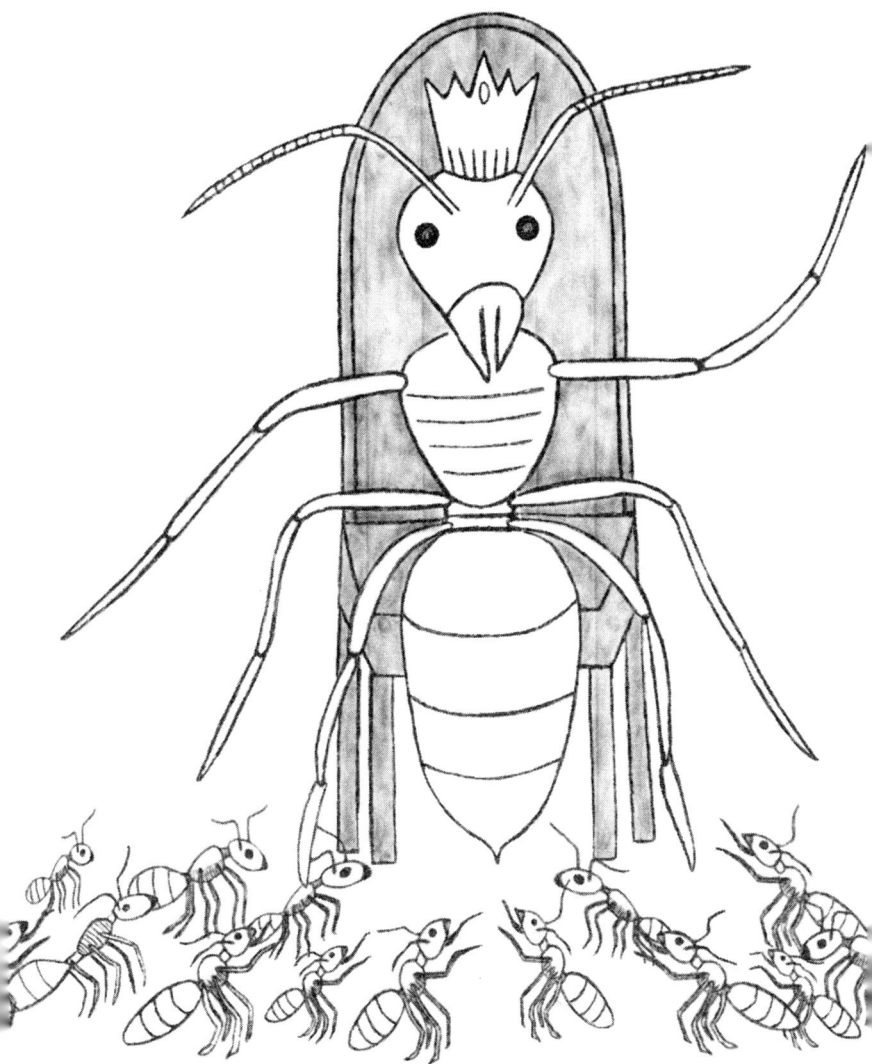

44 Axolotl in a Bottle

National ANThem

O Queen Antonia,
We love and worship ya,
Antonia.
You are the very best,
We've built the biggest nest.
Made a great throne for ya,
Antonia.

Dwelling in this great wood,
You rule our neighbourhood.
You are our star.
We will protect you, dear,
You'll never suffer fear.
You'll reign for years and years,
Antonia.

When old woodpecker comes,
We'll bite his eyes and bum,
He'll fly afar.
We'll be victorious,
Happy and glorious.
Your light shines over us,
Antonia.

Justin Case

Justin Case
Carried an umbrella
Just in case.

Justin Case
Never walked under a ladder
Just in case.

Justin Case
Never looked at a gorilla
Just in case.

Justin Case
Turned his nose up at paella
Just in case.

What more could he do
To stop things going wrong?
It is such a shame
He was put upon.

It came out of the blue
A cow fell from the sky
From an aeroplane.
What a way to die.

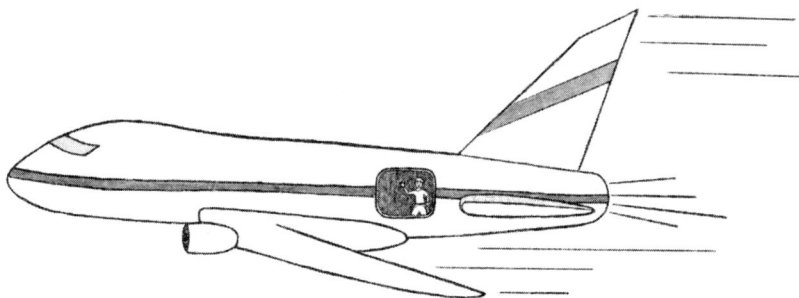

It squashed him flat
And that was that.

Justin Case
Wouldn't see a fortune teller
Just in case.

Justin Case
Should have stayed in bed forever
Just in case.

48 Axolotl in a Bottle

Beth's Brother Bert

Beth's brother Bert collected stuff,
He could never ever, ever, ever, get enough.

A strange-shaped stick stuck in the ground,
A round flat stone? He took them home.

Out in all weathers searching for feathers,
Sheep skulls, snail shells, ring pulls, cowbells.

He filled his pockets and carrier bags.
He filled the house with stacks of swag.

Their home was chocker, cluttered with clobber
You'd call tat. No room to swing a cat.

Beth's brother Bert was in seventh heaven.
He was as happy as Larry, he was fifty-seven.

Beth squirreled away just like her sibling.
She collected books by Rudyard Kipling.

Her hobby horses blocked the stairs,
Potato guns spilled off the chairs.

Beth loved her brother. They still lived together
With Bart and Barbara, their father and mother.

But 'twas time to get a lock-up, they'd run out of
   room.
Bert tidied up, Beth searched for a broom.

Their house needed to be shipshape. They gave it
   a spring clean,
Soon, arriving from the scrapheap would be a
   submarine.

With just a bit of tinkering, with just a lick of
   paint,
Bart and Barbara's project was to renovate

The ocean-going vessel, to restore it to its prime.
All the family worked together, and they had
   such a brilliant time.

Limerick Written In Norwich

There once was a man who lacked courage
Unless he ate potfuls of porridge.
When he'd gulped down the last
Of his oaty breakfast
He conquered the city of Norwich.

Hi Huw Haiku

'Hi Huw,' greeted Su,
'This is my haiku to you.'
'Thank you, Su,' said Huw.

Atchoo! Haiku

It's cool if you sneeze
When you're whizzing on your skis
As your snot will freeze.

Fish Tanka

An anemone,
To mighty fish in the sea
Ain't an enemy.

But small fry in the ocean
Might have another notion.

Limerick Not Written In Norwich

An ocelot got in a spot
After falling asleep in a pot.
It got warmer and warmer
As hot as a sauna
It got from that pot like a shot.

The Sparrow From Harrow

Archie Lea liked archery,
He loved his bow and arrow.
Stan did not, unfortunately,
Because he was a sparrow.

Tracking Stan from tree to tree
Archie'd not let him rest.
Silently and stealthily
He stalked him to his nest.

He drew the bowstring to his ear
And aimed at where Stan sat.
The arrow whistled through the air ...
Missed Stan, but killed the cat.

Octopus Rumpus

Our octopus caused a rumpus
Octavia truly shocked us
She clambered out of the fish tank
When she'd run out of creatures to eat
She slopped and squished across the floor
Scuttling towards the refrigerator
Her suckers stuck on the white metal door
When who should trot in from the street
But Stan the cat, well fancy that!
And fancy that she did.

Octavia then burped like a frog
A surprising sound for a cephalopod
But she had no time for satisfaction
No chance to savour a slow digestion
For her belch awoke our faithful hound
Who dashed downstairs and with one bound
Doug leapt upon our octopus
At precisely 8 o'clocktopus.

What followed was calamitous
He sank his fangs into her flesh
She thrashed, Doug slashed
And she, with such tenacity
Struggled towards her sanctuary
Doggedly Doug harried while carried
She dragged Doug up the table leg
Into a watery grave
Doug did not give up
Our Dougie was so brave.

They splashed into the aquarium
And that was the end of the both of them
Doug's final act before he drowned
In a fish tank black with ink
Was a fatal wound to Octavia
Which I'm sure you'll all concur
For such belligerent behaviour
'Twas only right and proper.

Oh, and just to say
Someone reported this to the RSPCA
Will they let us have another pet?
No way!

Kat's Cat?

Kat wanted a cat.
Dad said, 'No.'
Kat went to her room
Grabbed a felt-tip pen.
It squeaked as she scrawled on her bedroom wall.

Hand gripped tight,
Tongue thrust out,
Doodling done.
She purred at her picture.
The scribble mewed, 'Miaow'.
Then flopped to the floor
And scampered to the kitchen.

'Where did that come from?' asked Dad.
'I made it myself,' Kat proclaimed proudly.
'Did you? It's really, really, good.
What is it?'
'It's a cat.'
'Of course it is.'
'Can we keep it?'
'I don't see why not.'

When Mum came home
She said, 'What's that tat sat on the mat?'
And promptly put it in the bin.

Two Tigers And A Tabby Cat

Two tigers saw a tabby cat
Creeping by their cage.
They dashed over to gobble it,
But then became enraged.

The tabby, though, just stood there,
It didn't run away.
The look it gave the angry pair
Seemed to me to say,

'I was wild once, just like you,
But now I'm mild and tame.
I come and go from this old zoo,
And you can't—that's a shame.

But I'd swap places if I could,
Because I'd rather see
You escape into the woods,
Wild and running free.

For I'm a prisoner as a pet
I'm in captivity.
My ancestors would so regret
What's become of me.

I'd prefer your prison chains
To my sofa, that's for sure.
I so wish I could be untamed,
I'd roar like you for evermore.'

The tigers now were so het up
But could not reach their prey.
A keeper came and picked it up
And carried it away.

Two tigers and a tabby cat
Are all somewhere they hate.
They live in a lame habitat.
They share the same sad fate.

Awkward Orca

I'm an awkward orca
I'm not a manic marine marauder
I prefer a corner
Not particular about the Arctic
I prefer it warmer
Don't like swimming with the pack
That's not where I'm at
I want to make my home
Somewhere on my own
Don't refer to me as Killer Whale
I prefer to be a 'Chiller Whale'
And I really feel
I'd like to date a seal
I just hope none of the others
Choose to make this a big deal
That they don't make a meal
For if they do I'll blubber
If she's eaten by my brother.

Cool Cave Kidz

Come round to our house,
Come and play with us.

We live in Torquay,
Right beside the sea.

This is our wolf cub,
Watch him fetch this club.

My name is Pog,
My sister, she's called Zog.

First let's catch a fish,
That would be delish.

That will be our lunch,
Something good to munch.

We live in some caves,
Right beside the waves.

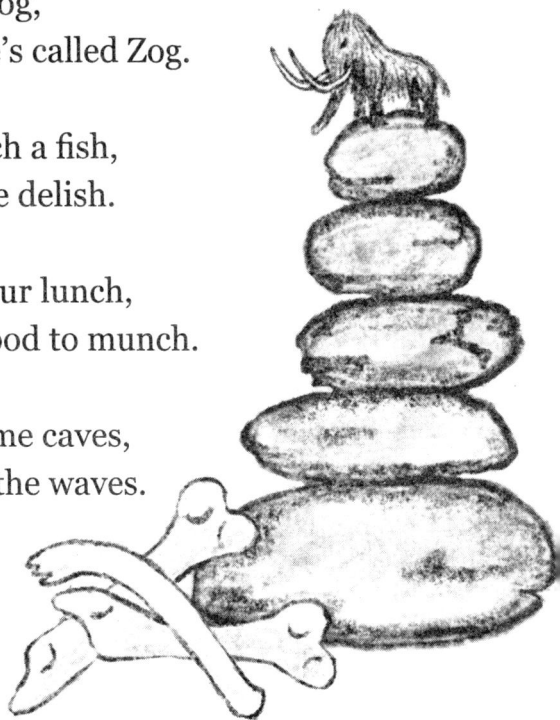

It is cool and cosy,
Come and have a nosey.

From the roof hang stalactites,
From the floor grow stalagmites.

It can be quite damp,
A bit like when you camp.

Let's sit by the fire,
That will make us drier.

See those white bones over there?
This was once a cave bear's lair.

You can dress in animal skins,
Wear a hat that's made of wings.

Make a necklace out of shells,
Smear ashes on your face as well.

Make music out of sticks and stones,
Blow loudly into mammoth bones.

Stomp like rhinos, sing like seals,
Grin like hyenas, wriggle like eels.

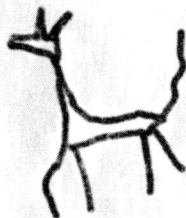

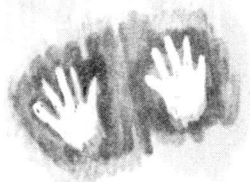

Let's paint pictures on the wall,
Then climb the cliffs—Watch out!—Don't fall!

At night we sleep upon the floor,
It's very draughty, there's no door.

Now that we've become good friends,
We could meet up soon again.

Next time we could come to your house,
Do you think your mum would like us?

Jellyfish On Toast

Sandy craves for candy floss,
Nick and Rory love knickerbocker glories.
Rocky snacks on sticks of rock,
Trish and Pip like fish and chips.

My dad goes for cockles,
My mum, she loves mussels.
But the treat for me when I'm on the coast,
So exquisite, it's delicious, is jellyfish on toast.

Jellyfish, jellyfish is delish,
It's the dish, the dish for me.
Jellyfish, jellyfish—the dish I so relish,
When I'm beside the sea.

I like it for breakfast,
For brunch or for lunch.
I like it for supper,
I like it for tea.

It wibbles and wobbles
There on the plate.
It slips down a treat,
Once I ate eight!

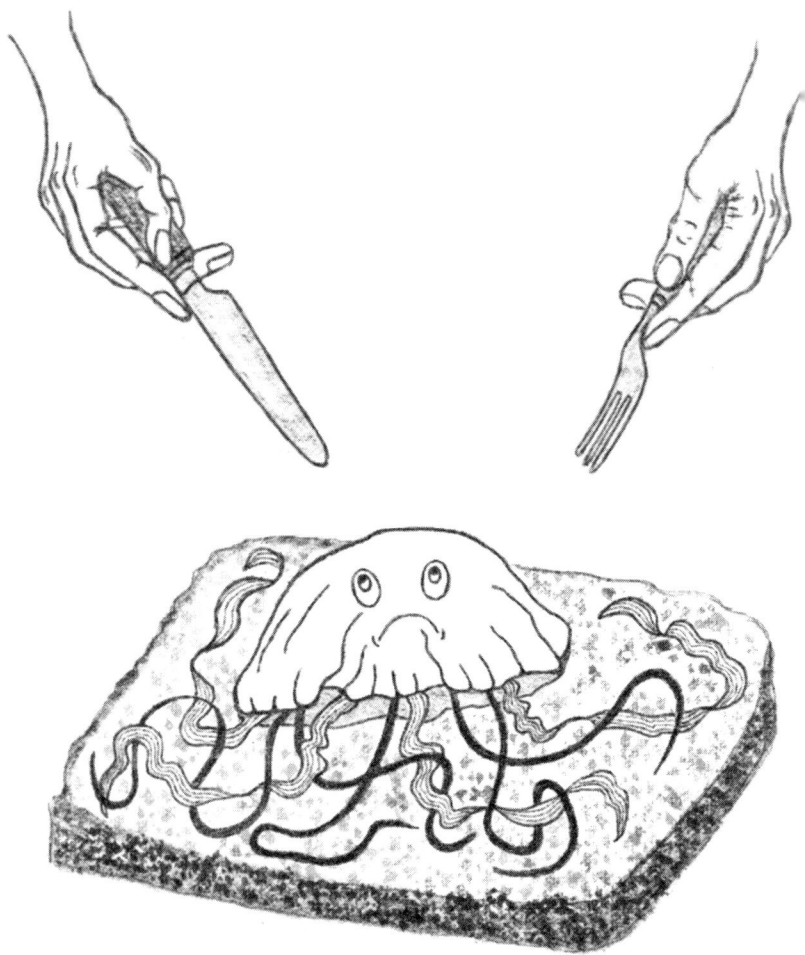

Jellyfish, jellyfish is delish,
It's the dish, the dish for me.
Jellyfish, jellyfish—the dish I so relish,
When I'm beside the sea.

Some say it's too smelly,
To put in your belly.
That it smells of wee,
But I don't agree.

Sure, it's an unusual flavour,
But I believe it's something to savour.
It tastes of the sea,
I eat it with glee.

Jellyfish, jellyfish is delish,
It's the dish, the dish for me.
Jellyfish, jellyfish—the dish I so relish,
When I'm beside the sea.

I don't want the usual
When I'm at the coast.
Just juicy jellyfish
On top of my toast.

It doesn't need salt,
Nor a sprinkling of pepper.
No mustard or ketchup
Just splashes of vinegar.

Jellyfish, jellyfish is delish,
It's the dish, the dish for me.
Jellyfish, jellyfish—the dish I so relish,
When I'm beside the sea.

When the fork goes in
It gives a little jiggle.
The bread goes soggy in the middle
But a hard dry crust is simply a must.

I like it for breakfast,
For brunch or for lunch.
I like it for supper,
I like it for tea.

Jellyfish, jellyfish is delish,
It's the dish, the dish for me.
Jellyfish, jellyfish—the dish I so relish,
When I'm beside the sea.

Seagulls Of Torbay

A seagull stole
Ike's ice cream,
Ike's ice cream,
Ike's ice cream.
A seagull stole Ike's ice cream,
When they went to Torbay.

A seagull stole
Pat's pasty,
Pat's pasty,
Pat's pasty.
A seagull stole Pat's pasty,
When they went to Torbay.

A seagull stole
Bill's burger,
Bill's burger,
Bill's burger.
A seagull stole Bill's burger,
When they went to Torbay.

A seagull stole
Sue's sun hat,
Sue's sun hat,
Sue's sun hat.
A seagull stole Sue's sun hat,
When they went to Torbay.

A seagull stole
Karl's car keys,
Karl's car keys,
Karl's car keys.
A seagull stole Karl's car keys,
When they went to Torbay.

A seagull stole
Flo's flip-flops,
Flo's flip-flops,
Flo's flip-flops.
A seagull stole Flo's flip-flops,
When they went to Torbay

A seagull stole
Tone's i-Phone,
Tone's i-Phone,
Tone's i-Phone.
A seagull stole Tone's i-Phone,
When they went to Torbay.

A seagull stole
Di's dolly,
Di's dolly,
Di's dolly.
A seagull stole Di's dolly,
When they went to Torbay.

A seagull stole
Finn's finger,
Finn's finger,
Finn's finger.
A seagull stole Finn's finger,
When they went to Torbay.

A seagull stole
Pip's puppy,
Pip's puppy,
Pip's puppy.
A seagull stole Pip's puppy,
When they went to Torbay.

Do Feed The Seagulls

Feeding the seagulls
They fly round and round.
Feeding the seagulls
They swoop up and down.
Feeding the seagulls
In the middle of town.
Feeding the seagulls
In the playground.

Never been to the zoo,
Never been to the fair.
Never been to the beach,
Never been anywhere.

Mum's got no money
So we always stay home.
It's too dangerous outside,
I play on my own.

We live on the top floor,
I stand on the chair.
I see the blue sea,
I want to go there.

When I went to school
They gave me free meals
And that's the reason
I had to steal.

I took a sandwich
From Sam's lunchbox
And I was caught
By Mr Fox.

Apples, biscuits,
Chocolate and crisps.
Wraps and rolls
And sandwiches.

I'd been sneaking food
To feed my mates
They'd cry as they'd fly
Over the grey school gates.

Feeding the seagulls
They flew round and round.
Feeding the seagulls
They'd swoop up and down.

Feeding the seagulls
I loved the sound.
Feeding the seagulls
In the playground.

Never been to the zoo,
Never been to the fair.
Never been to the beach,
Never been anywhere.

Why did I do it?
Sam's mum asked me.
I couldn't go to the sea
So I brought it to me.

Betty's Not A Yeti

There! There! There! There's a Yeti!
She ain't sweaty and she's not called Betty.

This ain't the Serengeti
She doesn't like spaghetti
But she enjoys poetry
But she thinks it's petty
Officially a crime
To write cheap rhymes
It's a waste of time
If there's no weight to the lines.

There! There! There! There's a Yeti!
She ain't sweaty and she's not called Betty.

Living in the Himalayas
Is the answer to her prayers
The wilderness
She likes best
She doesn't do cities
She doesn't like crowds
She lives in the mountains
With her head in the clouds.

There! There! There! There's a Yeti!
She ain't sweaty and she's not called Betty.

Playing hide and seek
At the roof of the world
You'll sometimes get a peek
Through the snow swirls
Leave your phone at home
Don't send up a drone
She just wants to roam
So leave her alone.

There! There! There! There's a Yeti!
She ain't sweaty and she's not called Betty.

Sometimes she appears
To mountaineers
Suffering from frostbite
And frozen tears
She'll give you a hug
To warm you up
She doesn't want your gratitude
Just get out of her altitude.

There! There! There! There's a Yeti!
She ain't sweaty and she's not called Betty.

The Swing

If you peek over the thorny hedge now
You'll see something occurring beneath the bough.
A swing is a-swaying, to and fro,
Rocking and swinging, high and low.

From a creaking branch, chestnut brown
A dangling seat arcs up and down.
A swing is a-swaying, to and fro,
Rocking and swinging, high and low.

There's no wind a-blowing, no summer breeze
Yet still hear the rustling, whispering leaves.
A swing is a-swaying, to and fro,
Rocking and swinging, high and low.

Nobody lives in that house anymore
Nobody has a key for the door.
A swing is a-swaying, to and fro,
Rocking and swinging, high and low.

Windows are boarded like eyelids nailed shut
Pondweed floats in the water butt.
A swing is a-swaying, to and fro,
Rocking and swinging, high and low.

Nobody lives in that house anymore
Nobody has a key for the door.
A swing is a-swaying, to and fro,
Rocking and swinging, high and low.

There's no wind a-blowing, no summer breeze
Yet still hear the rustling, whispering leaves.
A swing is a-swaying, to and fro,
Rocking and swinging, high and low.

From a creaking branch, chestnut brown
A hanging seat arcs up and down.
A swing is a-swaying, to and fro,
Rocking and swinging, high and low.

If you peek over the thorny hedge now
You'll see something occurring beneath the bough.
A swing is a-swaying, to and fro,
Rocking and swinging, high and low.

King of the Bouncy Castle

A new boy came to school
We thought he was a fool.
We saw him first thing Monday
He moved in such a funny way.

Wibbly-wobbly
Hibbledy-hobbledy
Knees were knobbly
Clothes not properly
About to topple-ly.

A new boy came to school
He broke all the rules.
When he turned up Tuesday
Our teacher looked on in dismay.

Battered backpack
Tattered anorak
Shirt not tucked in
Bits of baked beans
Smudge of mustard
Spattered custard
Broken pencils
Tattooed stencils

Toothpaste stains
Eyes like shattered windowpanes.

We missed him on Wednesday and on Thursday
The teacher hoped he'd gone away.

But we're very pleased to say
He came in late on Friday
And told us why he looked a mess
Have you any idea? Can you guess?

He lives in a bouncy castle,
Bouncy castle, bouncy castle.
He lives in a bouncy castle,
Boing! Boing!! Boing!!! Boing!!!! Boing!!!!!

It's hard to clean your teeth
Or keep in your seat
If all the time you're bouncing.
Boing! Boing!! Boing!!! Boing!!!! Boing!!!!!

If your house shakes like jelly
How do you watch the telly
If all the time you're bouncing?
Boing! Boing!! Boing!!! Boing!!!! Boing!!!!!

If you never keep still
It can make you ill
If all the time you're bouncing.
Boing! Boing!! Boing!!! Boing!!!! Boing!!!!!

How to do your homework
When the table makes your hand jerk
If all the time you're bouncing?
Boing! Boing!! Boing!!! Boing!!!! Boing!!!!!

And when you're in your bed
The ceiling bangs your head
If all the time you're bouncing.
Boing! Boing!! Boing!!! Boing!!!! Boing!!!!!

And I'll leave you to guess
Why the bathroom's such a mess
If all the time you're bouncing.
Boing! Boing!! Boing!!! Boing!!!! Boing!!!!!

He asked us if we'd come and play
And so, we went round Saturday,
And now we go there every day.
Boing!

Boing!!!!

Boing!!!!

Boing!!!!

Boing!!!!

Little Green Devils

Sing to the tune of Jingle Bells.

Brussels sprouts,
Brussels sprouts,
Put them on your plate.
They're not that bad
It makes them sad
That they're the ones you hate.

Brussels sprouts,
Brussels sprouts,
Don't reject in haste.
Don't live in fear
Of a once a year
Flavour that you taste.

If you've got a cough,
If you have a sneeze,
Here's a remedy,
Don't scoff, I beg you, please.
Don't turn green or pout,
Please just hear me out.

Packed with vital vitamins,
Better than a mandarin.

(It shouldn't be shocking
To find one in your stocking.)

Brussels sprouts,
Brussels sprouts,
Brussels all the way.
Oh, how healthy you would be
If you ate them every day.

Brussels sprouts,
Brussels sprouts,
Brussels all the way.
If you won't eat one
You'll not get your treat on Christmas Day.

Suzanne Loved A Snowman
Part 2

Suzanne loved a snowman
They liked to kiss and cuddle
But then her heart was broken
He left her in a puddle.

She brought him home to warm him up
And gave him Christmas dinner
But then she had to mop him up
When he'd become much thinner.

She poured his essence in a box
Then laid her lover in the freezer
She closed the lid on one top bloke
A really, well cool geezer.

She chopped the carrot and chomped upon
His handsome orange nose
His arms she planted in the garden
Hoping trees might grow.

His eyes she placed upon a shelf
Two lumps of jet-black coal
So, every time she stares at them
He sees into her soul.

Toss A Little Something In The Busker's Hat

Ladies, gents, others, girls and boys,
Come gather round and enjoy.
There's music on the streets and juggling too.
Spectacular feats just for you.
So, watch and listen, ooh and aah.
OOH! AAH!
We put ourselves on the line,
We open our hearts
To give you a good time.
So, please support the arts.

Chorus
If you like what you see,
You laugh and clap.
That makes us happy,
But we want better than that.
Dig deep into your pockets,
Then *we'll* laugh and clap.
If you toss a little something in the busker's hat.
(We'd fancy that!)

Toss in silver, chuck in gold,
It's a bottomless pit—a great big hole.
Pitch in some bread and cheese, a bottle of wine,
Spread a blanket and we'll dine.
Let's have a picnic on the streets.
It's hungry work and we need to eat,
And so once more, I repeat ...

Chorus
If you like what you see, etc ...

Passers-by of this pavement stage,
I hope you all have been engaged
And we've managed to build up a great rapport,
After all, that's our job, it's what we're here for.
So, show your appreciation generously,
We'll accept our reward graciously.
On the streets there is no pension scheme,
When winter comes, times are lean.

Chorus
If you like what you see, etc ...

Roof Preeder

Roof Preeder
Carnt splle vry wel
Gnaw kan eye
Butt eye kneed herr
2 reed lis po M
2 chek le punchooashun
Coz eye dnt no wear le kommas
Ore ful stpz ore squeschun marx shld b
Doo u

Karen Thwaite, aka *Krafty Karen,* lives not a million miles away from Mr. PiG and is a dab hand at interpreting Clive's imaginings. Like him, she's constantly creating one way or another—daubing, doodling, stitching, sketching, etching, knitting and playing with clay. Karen particularly enjoys constructing abstract ceramic sculptures and exhibiting them in the garden for all our feathery friends to perch upon and fill the air with glorious birdsong.

Andrew Kingham has made pictures using everything from metal biscuit tins to cardboard cereal boxes. He even uses pencils and paints sometimes, but he uses a computer to design Clive PiG's books because it would take too long to cut all the letters out by hand. Visit him at *www.andrewkingham.co.uk*

These illustrated paperback books particularly appeal to 5–11 year-olds, and some even younger, and many who are older.

The Adventures of Mister Storyfella contains twelve tip-top tales from around the world retold by Clive, featuring Señorita Catalina, Falak's Flutes, and The Man Who Turned Into A Volcano.

£5.99
Published by
PiGasus Publishing UK
ISBN 978-1-7397040-0-1

Book

Jurassic Cove & Other Jolly Japes is a humorous collection of Clive's stories, poems and wordy whatsamajigs, including Cosmic Barbeque, Anton Swallowed A Goldfish, Whirly Girly, and Exclamation Mark!

£5.99
Published by Caboodle Books
ISBN 978-0-9933000-8-0

Book

Book →

Unicorn In The Playground
is a compendium of Clive's
choicest cuts, including *Colin
the Chocolate Kid, Nice is
Nasty, Suzanne Loved A
Snowman, Our Dad's Not
Normal,* and *The Angry
Dormouse.*

£5.99
Published by Caboodle Books
ISBN 978-0-99548-853-3

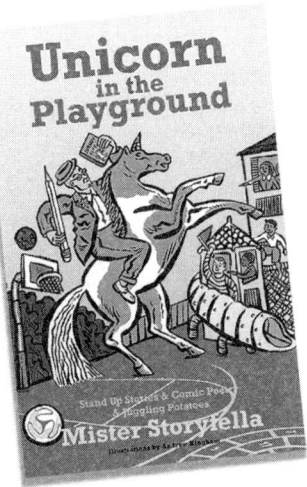

For small orders in UK please visit www.clivepig.co.uk/shop
For bulk orders and overseas sales please contact Caboodle
Books Ltd at info@caboodlebooks.co.uk

CD
←

Uncle Wolf – Music CD
Songs with a twist and tales
with teeth. Dark tales
humorously told. Only
suitable for those who dare
to say boo to a goose.

£5.99
Parental Guidance:
Suitable for ages 11–111.

QR code for →
the website

Chapter Twenty-Nine
The Treasure Reveal

After Angelle's ceremony, anticipation of opening the treasure chest had reached a fervour. At long last Jean-Baptiste, Evangeline, Lucky and Wellesley met privately at Lucky's warehouse to unseal the coffer. Morning coffee and pastries were served while waiting for Charlie, the head archaeologist. He would be responsible for photographing and cataloguing every single piece. Attorney Morgan also attended as a legal witness. He would be writing his own report to assure accuracy.

Lucky acquired the necessary drill bits and decided to do the honour himself. He used a cutting oil for lubrication making it easier to drill into the hard metal. Lucky held the noisy drill firmly as the spinning bit slowly dropped metal shavings unceremoniously on the floor. The monotonous drone got Jean-Baptiste to thinking about the marauding pirate crews that pilfered and plundered the high seas. From his studies, he knew the pirates were a rowdy bunch and tended to spend gold or silver quickly when in a port.

Try as he might though, Jean-Baptiste could not imagine that kind of reckless abandon of life and property. Pirating was a tough line of work that didn't last very long. Many were injured or killed during battle or fights. Pirates who committed a crime such as lying, cheating, stealing or fighting on board were punished several different ways. Depending on the infraction they could be marooned on an island, whipped, or even keel-hauled. Tied to a rope, the pirate was thrown overboard where he would be dragged down one side of the ship, under the vessel, over the keel and back up the other side. Ships bottoms were usually covered in barnacles, which caused bleeding and attracted sharks. Few survived this vicious punishment.

Evangeline put her arm around Jean-Baptiste and startled him back to reality, "Hey babe! What's up? You looked a million miles away."

"Oh! I was just thinking about what a hard life the pirates endured and what the history of this chest might be. I'm sure Jean Lafitte had all intentions of coming back for this treasure, but we don't really know what happened to him after he left for Texas. It seems his life and death are as mysterious as the swamps and bayous of Louisiana."

"Isn't it life's mysteries that intrigue us? We have an insatiable appetite to know the unknown," Evangeline replied.

"Yes, that's true! It's hard to imagine that kind of life driven by greed. Yet, in a weird sort of way, I can relate. It was a gamble they took on life and most lost. I know how desperation feels. I guess I'm not much different than them. I gambled too." He pulled Evangeline closer and smiled. "The only difference is, I won. I have you."

After burning through three drill bits, all the locks were finally removed. An almost reverent quietness filled the room as everyone anticipated opening the large ornate chest. Lucky said, "Jean-Baptiste, would you please do the honour?"

Flashbulbs fired as he raised the lid. Gasps went around the room as everyone gazed into the patinated copper-lined chest. A strange musty smell of ancient earth escaped into the room. A layer of sediment lay on top, diminishing the glow the stacked gold bullion bars and Spanish silver ingots. Charlie wore white cotton gloves as he carefully removed each piece for the cataloguing process. An impeccable Chinese porcelain Ming dynasty vase was carefully removed from the chest and meticulously cleaned.

Wellesley, who prided himself on information regarding the Ming dynasty, said, "I feel like a kid at Christmas. This blue and white patterned vase is stunning. This piece is probably from the 15th century when China was ruled by the powerful Ming dynasty. Look, the pattern is simple yet sophisticated. The element of cobalt was introduced during the reign of Xuande. It was cobalt oxide that gave Ming vases their beautiful blue nuances. This piece is in excellent condition considering its age and where it's been. This is unbelievable! Lucky, as you always say, we are witnessing history."

Wellesley immediately started researching Lucky's volumes on Ming dynasty pottery. Next, Charlie lifted a solid gold religious statue of the Virgin Mary with baby Jesus encrusted with numerous jewels. After photographing, Charlie wrote a description with dimensions and then registered it with a reference number. Lucky brushed the sediment off a stunning gold brooch inlaid with south sea pearls and adorned with a deep royal purple faceted amethyst surrounded with diamonds. Next, Charlie lifted a small bronze chest containing a large cache of escudo gold coins. Another petite bronze chest contained loose diamonds and valuable precious stones, mostly emeralds. Some were faceted and others remained in their natural state.

The silent reverence prevailed as everyone was in total awe of the moment. Lucky, who was grinning like a Cheshire cat, spoke with excitement, "This is exhilarating. I can hardly believe this is happening, yet it is. How fortunate are we to experience this time capsule. Wow! I'm just overwhelmed but so grateful to be sharing this adventure with all of you!"

Wellesley walked up to Lucky and gave him a big bear hug. "Lucky, that's the perfect name for you. You're right, this is unbelievable. I can't even begin to explain the emotions I'm feeling."

Once the chest was emptied, Evangeline's curiosity got the better of her. She observed that the inside depth of the chest seemed to be higher than the outside. She knocked on the floor of the chest and noticed a hollow echo. After scrutinizing the integral structure, she surprisingly discovered a false bottom. Carefully, Evangeline opened it with a sharp tool to expose an exquisite 17k emerald pendant set in 18k gold and accented with numerous diamonds of all sizes.

When Evangeline held the necklace up for all to see, Lucky's knees buckled and he grabbed the table for support. "Oh my God! Are you kidding me? This is the mother-lode. Evangeline, you are fantastic." Lucky retrieved his monocular handheld 10x magnification loupe to inspect the diamonds.

"Upon initial observation, these diamonds look to be a D-Colour which is the greatest quality. The cut looks to be old mine cushion cut with fifty-eight facets, and the clarity is amazing. These diamonds are exquisite, not to mention this stunning emerald. Wow!" Although he was ecstatic, he tried to maintain a certain decorum of cool. "No doubt this necklace previously belonged to royalty, perhaps a monarch from Spain or England. I'll have to contact my guy from Sotheby's in New York to find an accredited appraiser and track down the history of this piece. There's just no telling the value of all this. It might very well be priceless."

Every piece was photographed, given an ID number and catalogued. Descriptive cataloguing is time consuming, but allows for the organization of resources in a logical way, making information easy to find and understand. Lucky, an avid photographer himself, decided for security reasons to develop the film in his own darkroom. From there, Ethyl would compile the final report with one copy going to the State of Louisiana.

Lucky and Wellesley had made arrangements for 24-hour security inside and out. They even installed a new state-of-the-art security camera patented by Marie Van Brittan Brown.

Jean-Baptiste opened the back door for a breath of fresh air to discover the day was nearing sunset. He thought, *Where did the day go? I feel like I'm in a time warp.*

Wellesley also noticed the time and said, "My, what a productive day. I think we should all go out to dinner and celebrate. Let's freshen up and I'll have a limo pick us up in an hour. How does Commander's Palace sound?"

Cheers erupted and everyone applauded.

"Great, I will call and reserve a private room. There is going to be a press release tomorrow morning, so prepare yourself. This story is going national, even worldwide. Walter Cronkite's secretary called for an interview. Folks, this is big-time news."

Chapter Thirty
Everyone's Hero

Evangeline rose at dawn to witness the sunrise slowly filling the day with an ethereal light. She loved the early morning when she could be alone without interruption for an hour to work on her memoir titled, *Pieces of a Puzzle.* She began the first chapter with Angelle's story and wove the synchronicity of her life's events as though weaving a tapestry into a crescendo that told an even larger story of a witch, pirates and treasure. Ideas swirled through her brain and she wanted to capture the thoughts on paper before forgotten. She had been thinking, *Sometimes you have to dredge up the truth from secrets better left in the dark. You dredge your past as if it were buried treasure. Sometimes all you get is a chest full of rocks, but sometimes you get gold. That alone is worth the dredging.*

Evangeline glanced at the date on the calendar. *Geez, it's hard to believe that it's April 19th, 1974. My, how time has flown.* Jean-Baptiste and the twins were still sleeping soundly. After writing a couple of paragraphs, she took a sip of hot ginger tea and stretched. *I'm not very motivated to write this morning, but I do like that bit of inspiration I received. I'll just sit here and be grateful for the silence.*

Evangeline smiled as she gazed upon her favourite photo of Jean-Baptiste as the Mardi Gras King of Endymion toasting Mayor Landrieu at Gallier Hall. What a fun night as the crowd chanted, "Throw me something, Mister." In her wildest dreams, she never imagined the life they're living. The lights momentarily flickered and her attention turned to the antique crystal chandelier. It hung from a high ceiling that was accented with ornate crown moulding. Evangeline never conceived herself living in a house this fine. A sentimental tear of gratitude escaped down her cheek.

She gazed out the window of her office into the courtyard of their lovely, Governor Nichols Street home. She had fallen in love the first time she saw it. Constructed in 1828, the house proudly exhibits fourteen-foot ceilings, original wooden floors, venetian plaster and old exposed brick walls. With the stunning grand staircase, Evangeline thought of the house as a combination of historical charm and modern conveniences. The lush tropical and private courtyard that encompassed a small swimming pool, had become her favourite place to write. Water from a beautiful old copper wall fountain cascaded into the pool from the mouth of a mythical fish, creating a pleasing sound.

Evangeline decided to awaken Jean-Baptiste for they had a busy day planned. With pride, she looked at her husband's handsome face and brushed the hair out of his eyes. He had been working so hard. After being Lucky's protégé for two years, Jean-Baptiste had been surprised when Lucky offered him a partnership in the antique business. Lucky had taught them a lot about the importance of building a career and investing their wealth for the future.

Evangeline's wedding bouquet might have had some magic after all, as Lucky had plans to marry his high-school sweetheart. He decided the time had come to give up the bachelor life and to live his dream. He wanted to travel the world looking for unique antiques and collectibles, but he had not been able to leave except for brief periods. Jean-Baptiste had a natural business ability and would be a great fit to run the shop while he was away.

"Wake up, my love. We have a big day ahead, rise and shine," Evangeline cooed in Jean-Baptiste's ear.

He reached up and said, "Don't worry, I'll rise. Come here, ma cher. I need you right now. Nothing else is more important!"

Then they heard, "Mama!" That was the end of an intimate moment.

Evangeline pleaded, "Come on, Jean-Baptiste, get up. Help me with the kids. We've got to get ready for the dedication ceremony. Lucky will be picking us up in an hour."

Evangeline and Jean-Baptiste figured they had conceived the twins while on their honeymoon in Paris. Angelle Chloe and Austin Caleb were born on 1 April 1970 and had recently celebrated their fourth birthday. The twins had become more socially active with other kids, allowing for Evangeline to have time to write her book and help Rosie run a shelter for battered women. Evangeline loved being a mother, but she encouraged the twins to be independent and think for themselves. She always had fun helping them explore their amazing curiosities.

"Chloe, find your shoes. Come on, girl, we gotta go," Evangeline prodded. She looked at Jean-Baptiste with a look of exasperation, but he just smiled and mouthed the words, "I love you."

Caleb was whining because he wanted to bring his favourite stuffed animal which was larger than him. Daddy had told him "No" but that didn't carry as much weight as mama. Evangeline took control. "Whining is not allowed today, do you understand, cowboy? Now, let's go. This is a very special day for mommy and daddy and you are not going to spoil it." She tousled his hair and leaned down to tickle underneath his chin until he giggled. She could always make him laugh. After a frantic breakfast, finally, they were ready. The foursome tumbled out the door where Lucky greeted them. After a short ride to the wharf, they boarded a crew boat and headed out to the swamps.

Spectacular purple Louisiana irises greeted them as they pulled alongside the freshly built boardwalk. Evangeline loved the beauty and smell of the swamps and bayous, especially in springtime. She wanted her children to experience where she grew up too. Her old house had been torn down and Jean-Baptiste had built them a sweet little cabin. Weekends were never better as they taught Chloe and Caleb how to fish and catch crabs.

As the sun would set, Evangeline and Jean-Baptiste would have a cocktail and wet a line. It was their favourite part of the day. One evening, she leaned into Jean-Baptiste and whispered, "My love, we have the best of both worlds, the solitude of nature and the excitement of the city. I'm such a lucky girl."

The dedication ceremony of Swamp Witch Haddie's statue and Jean Laffite's State Park had made national news. The new park had five miles of boardwalks installed along with plaques telling the story of pirates, a witch and buried treasure. The story had captured the nation's imagination. Several news crews eagerly established their position attempting to get the best shot and coverage.

Lucky and Wellesley were chatting with Governor McKeithen, who said, "Boys, I sure wanna thank y'all for your generous donation to the state of the royal necklace, the religious statue and the priceless Ming dynasty vase. We're opening a permanent Jean Lafitte exhibit at the New Orleans Museum of Art and History. We also have an artist working on another bronze statue to honour Swamp Witch Haddie. It seems she's everyone's hero."

Wellesley responded, "You are welcome, sir. Those items are way too valuable not to share with the public. We are just honoured to have been a part of discovering a lost treasure."

"Governor, we are so proud to be a part of this moment in history. The synchronicity of events that lead to this occasion shows us that the truth is much stranger than fiction. This is a special day and I'm proud to live in the great State of Louisiana," Lucky added.

The governor's aide informed him it was time for his dedication speech. He walked confidently to the make shift stage. "Welcome, my fellow Louisianians. Thanks for your confidence in me. It's an honour to serve as your governor. Let's have a moment of silence and take in the beauty and history of this special place."

The crowd grew quiet for a minute before he continued, "We are so excited to be here and dedicate this new park in honour of Jean Lafitte and Swamp Witch Haddie. There are so many stories within these stories, but today I would like to introduce you to the young man originally responsible for the discovery of Jean Lafitte's buried treasure. Jean-Baptiste Landry, would you please step forward?"

Handsome Jean-Baptiste walked to the podium, grinning from ear to ear, and shook the governor's hand.

"Thanks, Governor. Welcome, everyone! Thanks for coming out for the dedication ceremony and to hear our story. Let's give a big hand to my love and inspiration, my beautiful wife, Evangeline. Without her and my partners, Lucky Leroux and Wellesley Hyde, none of this would have been possible."

The crowd cheered loudly and Evangeline smiled shyly, not being a fan of the spotlight. Jean-Baptiste continued, "As our illustrious governor mentioned, there are so many stories within these stories, but the greatest story should belong to Swamp Witch Haddie. She was a very special being who silently lived among us. The lesson here for me and should be for all of us, is not to judge by appearances. Things are rarely what they seem.

"Just because we think someone is different than us, is not a reason to judge for the colour of their skin, religion or beliefs. Swamp Witch Haddie saved my life, in more ways than one. I owe her a great debt of gratitude. So, it is with great pleasure that I unveil and dedicate this beautiful bronze statue to my departed friend, Swamp Witch Haddie." Jean-Baptiste pulled back the canvas covering and flashbulbs fired simultaneously as photographers scrambled to get the best shot. The large crowd cheered with great enthusiasm. "Now it's time to celebrate! Les Bon Temp Rouller!"

Clifton Chenier teasingly played blues licks on his beautiful accordion, kicking off a rowdy set of Zydeco music with the Louisiana Ramblers. The young folks starting dancing passionately while the older folks lined to up enjoy the delectable feast that lay before them. The spicy smell of boiling crawfish permeated the air. It was a Cajun Fais do-do that would no doubt go into the night.

A striking young woman walked up to Evangeline and extended her hand with a business card. "Hi, I'm Ann Leroux. I heard that you are writing a book and I would love to offer my help. Previously, I was a professor of literature at Tulane. I'm now an agent and have several publishing companies that I have successfully submitted manuscripts to."

Evangeline started to respond when Chloe pulled on her skirt. "Mama! Mama!"

Evangeline looked down at Chloe. "Hush, child! I'm having a conversation. Don't you remember how rude it is to interrupt someone while they're talking?"

"But... But... Mama! Who is dat woman over there dat keep smiling at me? See her? She got shiny eyes, mama. She look just like that statue."

The End